Lang may yer
lum reek! ☺
Big love & blessings
Rara
xxx

Arisaig

Poems by Chris Waters

Happy Birthday
to a special
f
Suzanne

Happy Birthday
Caroline
Memories of a special
Place for a special
friend.
love Sarah xx

Happy Birthday
love
Lauren

mudlark

First published by Mudlark Press 2010
in a limited edition of 300
© Chris Waters 2010

ISBN 978-0-9565162-0-6

Printed in Exeter by Short Run Press Ltd
Cover and design by Sally Chapman-Walker

Published and distributed by
Mudlark Press, Littlehempston, Devon
www.mudlarkpress.co.uk

For Sandra,

Ben and Dan,

and the memory of my mother.

'For our house is open, there are no keys in the doors
And invisible guests come in and out at will'.

Czeslaw Milosz
'Ars Poetica'

For the words, too, to fly –
like these swallows,
fledged from dark angles
in rafters and eaves,
arriving in their own time
with the fine dust of distances,
their high risk wind-ride,
their lift and spin
breasting the air, then
flickering for purchase
at gable stones,
before aiming, laser-sure,
into the waiting space
of the barn – home.

Unpacking my books
on to new-painted shelves,
a pang of pleasure
as Basho returns,
home from the North,
to sit a while
on this ledge of fresh snow.

On the window-shelf
green against massed grey rain-cloud
three hyacinth shoots

Shimmer of midday
grasses in an unmown field –
shadows of old oaks

Late September after-rain light
cider sharp on the apple trees –
darkness only hours away

March rains spike the pond,
and again the night-frogs
have returned, their thin cries
urgent, guttering in the dark:
the surface buckles with their fusings –
by morning the eggs are all inscribed.

Wind-skimmer, airy
sky-rider, death
has slowed you
into this stiffened arc,
a final learning curve,
but the double crescent
of your folded
fledgling wings has me
searching for the muted,
consolatory vowels in
angelus and *quietus*,
and picturing Saharas,
snow-peaks and the bright,
beckoning constellations
encoded within
your little eggshell skull.

Not long after Neruda died,
an eagle flew into his room
and landed at his desk:

when you died I spent
days on the lookout,
scanning for consoling signs.

I can confirm
that one of your geese limped,
dragging her wing

and that the other stretched
her neck skyward to swallow
water, sipped from the pan;

six pheasants appeared
in their russet mandarin silks,
filing through your long grass;

two starlings on our roof crest
faced your house, beaks alert,
the sun sheening their breasts.

A distant buzzard idled high
but swallows were already
a memory on the empty wires.

The first leaves shrivelling;

black glint of elderberries

in the hedge; late pears

holding out against the drop –

darkness whistling from the North.

I watched a gull, reflected in glass,

cut a white arc across a dark screen;

detached from its cry, it floated skywards –

so, in memory, you arrive – then pass.

That flame may draw flame

and light engender light

we burn this candle

through your longest night.

Fear – again:

here,

in the mute heart,

deaf,

remorseless –

as an adder

coils

a cold stone.

In unfinished night
snow woke me from the colder dream:

I swam against a tilted sky –
blizzard of stars, flakes, lost faces,

all white, and so many crying.
The lantern stammered out of sight.

Awake, the black minutes ticked
while cries repeated on the hill:

I shouldered harness, sacking, rope –
unlatched the door at first light.

Is where she lives,

the quilt of fields blown up and back

by the sea-winds;

where she sleeps –

verticals and horizontals straining

in uneasy truce;

where she dreams,

and the black-sailed sloop drops anchor

beneath a bald moon;

when she wakes,

she paints sunrise on a canvas

before the light breaks.

Picasso in his high sea-tower
tastes the breeze of turquoise day:
as the white yacht skiffs through foam
(curlicue, arabesque, serif)
his pencil skims the page's bay.
Look – how simply we are drawn naked,
how swiftly the old bearded demi-gods –
centaur, satyr, shy minotaur –
arrive to ponder, tease, seduce, repose:
the stilled white yacht idles on the tide.

Elsewhere, the Fuhrer, Primo, Duce
are plunging their big rollers into black wells,
into ditches of red: painting by numbers
fat pincer-columns, arrow-swathes,
that soak into the land like dye –
each brushmark daubing dust, rubble,
a smoking sky.

War Photographer
Robert Capa, 6 June 1944

Zig-zagging to outwit

death's flying metal

final moment impact,

he lunges through the assault,

over the dead and

the stumbled dying

to take, not a yard of sand

but this, this grainy now,

this roar of surf

and gunfire, this yelling

face, this frantic arm,

technicolour drained

to black and white,

coolly focussed, and

until the next moment, intact.

Indexed in a glass case
    the skull of an Infantryman reclines –

his life having escaped him,
    in a long-ago milli-second,

through a bullet-hole as neat,
    but not as broad, as a wren's egg,

and brushing *en passant* against
    the bloodied sleeve of the young

Field Surgeon, who had not, he noted,
    among his gleaming implements,

been issued with a sweep-net
    sufficiently broad – or fine –

to sieve the swirl of smoke and cordite
    for all these newly roiling souls.

Soldiers

'Yet why not say what happened?' – Robert Lowell

My grandfather's room was pipe-fumed,
spartan, orderly: the blanket squared,
the razor and comb positioned
ready for the next manoeuvre.
He wore thick flannel trousers
which bared his doll-pink prosthetics
at the ankles; his silver hair
was yellowed with a tobacco-streak.
His medals held the other colours,
stories of which he never spoke:
what else did he lose – or win – at Ypres
to earn such awesome rainbows?
He would load his pipe, then drift from us
to No-Man's-Land, swathed in silent smoke.

South-London would-be wide-boy, fly,
cocky in his tilted film star trilby,
my father didn't fancy the conscript life:
AWOL on his stolen honeymoon,
he was frogmarched back to action
by red-capped military police.
I wish his army pay-book that I'm holding now
told his story in his words: I know
the Army filed his teeth, taught him to box,
to drive trundling khaki war-machines,
and, somewhere in Italy, to taste fear.
When peace broke out on Civvy Street
 he came home, a joke in his de-mob suit,
disarmed, trigger-happy, primed to fight.

Late-season, and my mother is busy
bottling memory: time-steeped distillations,
decanted clear, then ranged in her cupboard dark:
the twenties, the thirties, the war years.
One jar, neatly labelled Blitz – *October*
1942 is heavy with dark glittering juices:
there is weeping here, rubble and dust –
a mother lost, a family splintered
on one casual, arbitrary night.
As she returns the jar to its waiting shelf,
I wish her free of it, after six decades,
or free at least to peruse it now
as a child's winter snow-glass,
where reversible flakes drift gently down.

Epitaph
for buried sailors, Pistil Meadows, Cornwall

'Narrow, this craft, and frail —
and the moon-bright sea so wide:

where is the rudder to guide me,
where the mast for my furled white sail?'

On a nest
of stripped winter twigs

in an arrow squint
of the wrecked tower

two eggs
bone white
and mother-flown

Her love came like snowfall
through the year's longest night –
a gathering, gentle stealth:
by morning the roof was crested
with an immaculate weight,
the windows streaming new light.

Her leaving was the blizzard
on that midnight train
hurtling across blurred borders:
insomniac, I opened
a window onto the blackness –
the soul-stinging cold
of snowflakes in wild flight.

Another year – and the wife
you chose to widow
is trying to plant bulbs
around the base of your slate headstone;

you would recognise the curse
she conjures for you as she wrestles
her trowel into the summer-baked clay.

Cigar smoke and mother-of-pearl:
this blind accordionist
teases a melody
that shifts like sea over sand:
he is holding her close again,
her spine ivory-cool
to his sideway hand.

Sky-flakes skim and craze
the river's dancing skin,
shifting tree-cloud-shapes
from their green mirrored glaze;

under bloom and refraction,
where currents run,
the anchored weed sways –
emerald, lengthened, defining
and re-defining its own perfection.

Walking, we come across
deserted stone-rows:

here are ground-lines,
walled shelter-shapes

of roughed granite stacked
shin high, nudged together,

penned in a huddle, soft
with sprung grass and brackens,

stone-shields of lintel and jamb,
hearth and doorway,

squared against moorland
rain-blast and cloud-blow:

silenced, we turn homeward,
while the wind, on an in-breath,
shifts through the ferns.

And sometime to cross again
in the red boat
over the swell of the Sound

to the island: to walk
again its springy turf,
to come at last

to the roofless farmhouse,
its gaping windows re-clarified
by evening light.

Cross to Great Island
      over Blasket Sound
and ask after those
      who draw the long net
for fish, and for words –
      salt sprats in barrels,
and time-worn tellings
      round the smoking hearth:

'Their boats slipped out
      on a falling tide
in the early light,
      and they are long away –
their roofs all open
      to the migrant wind,
their chimneys cold,
      each window hanging wide'.

Stooping to inspect

    furrows

in his stone-walled

    field

in long evening

    light,

a man and his

    shadow

seem companionably

    hinged.

That their reels
    might quicken
        slide the bow

strike the string
    let the ear
        find the note

of fiddlers
    long gone
        their patterns

all nimble
    in the heels
        on the boards.

We laced the pasta with transparencies
of garlic and airy pecorino,

rose and dipped with the black prow as it sliced
the light-flaked buoyancies of the lagoon.

'Every tourist camera devours a piece
of this damp and crumbling city

into the black hole of its lens' – you joked –
'no wonder the place is sinking'.

But where our eyes loved to linger –
on time-veined tessellations; on the cool calm

eyes of saints; on sun-swiped or ripple-lit
alabaster, Istrian or travertine,

why not say that something, some airy
insubstantial part of us remains,

some salve, some shaving, some *trucioli* –
I mean, just look at these cloud-lacings

in the white marble of our local church
that floats between light and water – *The Miracoli*.

Sitting for a Portrait
for Ashton Chadwick

I sit facing away
from the face
he is coaxing into shape

and hear the dry rustle,
the soft scrape
of thumbed shading.

All I have to do
is wait, and look out
beyond the middle distance

perhaps to where the light
glints on a patch
of dark horizon;

as he draws, he loosens
into memories, the years,
the dates, the marks

made or left undone,
the lamps lit,
and the flame that still beckons –

until, glinting clear
in the empty space before me,
from half a century back,
I see a Cornish farmyard, dry
with summer dust, and a delighted,
solitary cross-legged boy,
clasping new-laid, new-found eggs.

'You can look now', he says.

Far off, the lines between salt-marsh,
sea, and sky are pure horizontals,
November-lit, shading softly
through oyster, to sable, then slate;

but here, in the silt creeks, they loop,
liverish, intestinal, in channels
that glisten at low tide
with the day's soft ingestings.

Verticals are in short supply:
a stand of poplars, airbrushed on a rise;
the dark lozenge of a house
against a distempered sky;

and the one figure, sloped
into a headwind, silhouetted
where the levee seems to shimmer —
a brush-stroke, a glyph, a grace-note
diminishing.

At Nice Airport

'Visitor Parking – Kiss and Fly'

All roads, and the day, grow wine-dark:
Our ways stretch before us, differently lit –
we will take the hill-massed, shoreline route,
and you, the convex nightways of the sky.

Odysseus, first among wanderers,
old way-weaver, night-watchman, hearth-hunter,
steady your lodestone, angle your eye,
shadow us, as we turn to kiss, part, fly.

Time-blackened city,
infested with footprints
and epitaphs,

voyeur of our daily
processions, connoisseur
of the singular histories

with which we are saddled
as we weave nomad steps,
unspooling silk-roads

and salt-trails
across your cracked,
finite streets.

I've kept two shells from Arisaig for you —

a razor and a mussel, bone-cool

and with a slight salt rasp to the touch,

light as the wind-scoured vowels and that final,

guttural catch in *Arisaig*, their sea-sky

creams and blues banded in pale accretions.

They came from that glittering white beach

we slid onto in our red kayaks, already

re-living the tilt and swell we'd paddled —

the shoreline piled with soft bleached siftings,

stone and bone minutiae of lived-out lives —

and our talk still live with our sightings:

the shark and seal-ways we'd intersected,

moments where the dark flicker of a fin,

or a moan echoing over pearled water

earthed us into pathways wilder than our own.

This stranded baleen —
slumped tonnage on the shore —
would hear kinship
in the drone and keening

of the bagpipes saluting
its loss — the squeeze
of swallowed air fingered
by the heart's lament;

and look — from its bloodfest
of galleried gore, the oil-skinned
worker appears, bearing the Grail
of its voice-box, anvil-huge,

its valves and vacant ducts
fingered now by our upper air,
that once sped speechings
aching across oceans.

The Memory of Apples
Great Chalfield Manor

The apple store —
tree-shaded,
flagstone-cool;

the door shuts
on an almost
churchy silence —

and dark
empty racks
where, from last summer,

just a few uglies
endure,
puckered and humble:

I am breathing
the memory
of apples,

their amber absence.

Moon-sallow
silver-eyed sister
swathed in a drift
of blue –
hour-sifter
uneasy sleeper
arrow-maker, lookout,
ember-keeper.

The Lark Ascending
for Benedict Rubbra

As when, waking
on a winter day
dark with rain,

spent breath
clinging
to the window glass,

we clear a porthole
in the mist,
and drawing with finger-tips,

speed droplets
into lines, and lines
into rivulets,

that race and shimmer
into filaments
of escaping light.

The astronomers perceive concentric rings:
my mappa mundi journeying is such
that all I know of *Terra Nova*,
Eldorado, the edge of *Finis-Terre*,
is this sawn, uneven, endless grainy touch.

Half-moon rising
golden
as the pheasant's eye;

Mars, manoeuvring
closer – fireblood
in the dawn sky.

When I wake from the dark,
bring me to this music
once again, this purling

song, trickling like a brook
through shadow, with sunlight
glancing off mottled rock.

And, for the afterlife,
what better emblem
than this Roman's choice,
carved on his corroded tomb:

a dolphin, companion,
spirit-guide, riding
the lethal waters,
arching, and driving a wash

that rocks the ferry, slow
and heavy on its nightly commute,
passengers pressed at the rail,
waving, their bleached eyes lit

one last time as we pass?

Acknowledgements

I would like to acknowledge the editors
of *Acumen* and *Poetry Scotland*, where
some of these poems first appeared.

Thanks go to Peter Bently, Bill Eaton and
Malcolm Ross for their helpful readings
of this collection in its early stages.

Special thanks to Sandra Greaves for
her generous time spent on editorial
questionings.

Finally, thanks to Sally Chapman-Walker
of Mudlark Press, whose patience and
creative vision have seen the book
through from the beginning.

'Arisaig' can be ordered through
www.mudlarkpress.co.uk